TEARS, FEARS, and CHEERS:
Ripples from Childhood

Veneta Shepherd

TEARS, FEARS, and CHEERS:
Ripples from Childhood

My great-grandparents didn't know how to read or write, so I don't have much family history. Their stories were never passed down. I have five amazingly wonderful kids and two incredible grandchildren. There will be many generations behind me. Now that I have grandkids, it has become important to leave some family history for the descendants that I will never meet. I want them to have some idea of who I was, and what life was like for me.

This is dedicated to them.

Forward

I am a Black woman, descended from Black men and women who were stolen from their countries, their homes, their families, for selfish and inhumane purpose. They were crowded onto ships with little food or water. They were stripped of their dignity, their language, their identities, and their culture. Many did not survive the trip. Those that did were strong and resilient.

Because they were so strong, they were whipped, beaten, and terrorized into submission. Despite back-breaking work all day, everyday, they owned nothing and were considered to be the legal property of their white "masters" for generation after generation. The "masters" and their descendants prospered mightily as the free slave labor built the economy of this country.

The first generation of slaves were kidnapped from their freedom and thrust into an evil world of hate and brutality. They knew what a life of freedom meant and felt like. That is the basis of the resilience that was passed down to generations that would only know a life of slavery. Through it all, Black people held tightly to the hope for a return to freedom for their own descendants. Against all odds, their strength and resilience survived.

None of this was taught to me in my history classes.

I tell myself that what pain I face now is nowhere near as bad as what my ancestors faced as slaves. I have to rationalize my "normal" so that I can continue to function, but I don't ever process the daily pain of racism. Pain and trauma are processed through perspective. I can't get enough distance from the everyday onslaught of racism to gain the necessary perspective. The only perspective I am afforded is that of my ancestors, and that pain is impossibly deep; too deep for my heart to hold.

The pain of my enslaved ancestors courses through my spirit, as does the pain that I witnessed as the Civil Rights Movement unfolded. Unprocessed pain gets passed down through generational dysfunction, and that was a theme with the women of my family.

Trauma and abuse were kept hidden in darkness, never exposed to healing light.

Memories are a process of zooming in on past events in our lives. Sometimes we focus on details that didn't stand out before. Some memories have deeper impact, creating ripples that affect us throughout our lives. It's hard to understand the significance of those events while we're in the midst of them. We need the gift of time and the willingness to zoom out to see the wisdom of a different and broader perspective.

Resiliency is not given. It is earned through figuring out how to hold on to what is most important during hard times. It's about finding the strength within to move through the darkness, always trusting that there is light ahead. Acknowledge the pain, but do not surrender to it. Surviving one hard time lays the foundation of courage and faith to survive the next hard time. Struggle creates appreciation for the goodness of life. Each struggle also carries gems of beauty deep within that reveal themselves as perspective changes and wounds heal.

The Civil Rights Movement played out in the background of my childhood. I didn't understand the significance while I was growing up in the middle of it, but I could sense the triumphs and the tragedies. Walk with me in my childhood shoes as the Civil Rights Movement unfolded around me.

6 MONTHS OLD WITH MY GRANDMOTHER

Early Childhood Ages 3-5

I was born on July 29, 1954, and lived in the southern section of Minneapolis MN all of my life. I'm the oldest of seven. My four brothers are right behind me, and my two sisters are the youngest. There were no cell phones or computers when I was a kid, most TV shows were in black and white, and kids played outside until it was too dark to see.

We were on the lower end of middle class. There was always enough food, although it was not necessarily "healthy" food. The lights and heat were never turned off. We bought clothes once a year from the massive

Sears catalog, and shoes once a year from Robert's Shoes.

We never rode a plane as a family, and we saw one movie together, well, two (it was a double feature), Lady and the Tramp, and 101 Dalmatians. We had one family car until I got my license and got a decent used car from my Dad. The bills got paid, but there was very little cushion. We are fiercely loyal to each other, and, like most families, there are things we never talk about.

On Aug 28, 1955, 14-year-old Emmett Till was brutally murdered for supposedly flirting with a white woman. His mother refused to hide the brutality of her son's murder, and insisted that his casket lay open for all to see. That image was published in the Black magazine, Jet, and later published around the world. Emmett's murderers were acquitted, and decades later, the woman who accused him recanted her story. This was, and in many ways still is, the reality of the justice system for Black people.

A few months later, as Rosa Parks sat in the first row of the Black section of a bus as the bus began to fill with white people. The driver moved the sign indicating the Black section further back and told Rosa Parks she had to move. She refused to give up her seat, not because she was tired from work, but because she was tired of being disrespected and treated unfairly, and being told where she could and could not be. She was arrested and hauled off to jail.

These two incidents helped mobilize resistance to segregation, laying the foundation for demonstrations and marches that would grow into the Civil Rights Movement. This was the backdrop of my childhood.

My earliest memory is being in the kitchen of the home I shared with my parents and little brother. I was about 3-years-old, and my brother was about one, sitting in a high chair. I believe we lived in the top floor of a duplex, because I remember walking up the outside back stairs all the way to the top. The kitchen is the only thing I remember about that place. I have no memories of any other rooms or activities.

Truthfully, I really only remember one scene from that time in my life. We were all sitting at the kitchen table eating a meal, and my parents were discussing moving to a different place; specifically, a bigger apartment versus buying a house. My mother was pregnant and we needed more space. It seemed as though Dad was in favor of the house, and Mom was in favor of the apartment. He was more adventurous and free-spirited, while she was more reserved and resistant to big changes.

I remember this particular scene because their conversation felt more intense than any I had heard before. Frankly, it scared me a bit. I don't recall ever hearing them argue before, or since, actually, so it was very uncomfortable for me, particularly when they asked me what I thought. It felt like I had to choose a side.

The thought of moving to an actual house sounded fun and exciting, especially with the promise of having my own room. To be fair, that kitchen was very small. I had to stand up and move my chair if someone needed to get into the refrigerator during a meal. I didn't want to hurt my Mom's feelings, but it was just too hard to contain my three-year-old enthusiasm and curiosity, so it was pretty clear which side I chose. I saw the fear and resignation pass across my Mom's face, and that's all I remember. We moved to an actual house a few weeks later.

As promised, I got my own bedroom, and another baby brother arrived soon after we moved. I have lots of memories about that house, some good, some not so good. Most of the not-so-good memories involve my Mom.

ME AT ABOUT 9 MONTHS OLD - IN "THE DRESS"

Whenever my Mom would show me a certain picture
of me as a baby, she would tell me the story of the

dress that I'm wearing in the photo. She said that my Dad bought it for me in Korea when he was on his way home after being discharged from his Army service. She told me that the dress cost a lot of money, and she couldn't return it because it came from Korea. She seemed to enjoy telling the story, because I heard it many times, but she told it with such bitterness and resentment, and that deeply confused me.

I still don't know how to react to this story, and I haven't figured out her intention for telling it to me. Was I supposed to feel guilty? Angry at my Dad for buying a present for me? Did she expect sympathy? Was she expressing her resentment toward me? Toward my Dad? Her expectations were difficult to understand.

We always had a rocky relationship. I never felt like she loved me. I don't even think she liked me. She told me several times that she had always wanted a boy baby first, so I felt like I was a huge disappointment to her and the life she had been dreaming of. Obviously, I couldn't change into a boy, but I could act more like a boy, which is exactly what I did. Honestly though, I thought girls were pretty boring anyway. I found that running and playing sports were WAY more fun and interesting than pretending that Barbie had a life.

We didn't have a lot of money, so I mostly played with paper dolls when it was too cold or rainy to be outside, but I never enjoyed it. They were so delicate, and something always got torn so things wouldn't work right, and I felt like I'd get in trouble for breaking something. It was just way too much stress. To this day, I don't know if I was doing "boy" things to try to gain her love and attention, or if that's who I always was anyway. I don't think it really matters anymore.

My Mom had a white friend that lived a few blocks from our house. This friend had kids around our age, so we all spent a lot of time hanging out together. One afternoon, Mom's friend was driving us home from some appointment. Mom was in the front passenger seat, my baby brother was sitting in her lap (this was WAY before seat belts), and my brother Bro and I were in the back seat. It was a gorgeous day, so we had our windows rolled down.

As we were driving up a hill, a car came over the top of the hill on our side of the street. We got hit on the front driver's side, and our car spun around a couple of times and hit a tree at the bottom of the hill. The impact with the tree propelled me out of the window and into the street.

I remember our car spinning and hitting the tree; I remember flying through the window, although I don't remember flying through the air. I remember laying in the street and seeing another car heading down the hill toward me. I wanted to move, but I think the wind had gotten knocked out of me because my body was stuck for a minute. A white couple asked if I was okay, and helped me walk to our wrecked car to see how my family was.

An ambulance took us to the hospital. Mom's friend and my brother Bro were uninjured. Mom had a cut on her nose from my baby brother's head. My knee got banged up pretty badly, and I ended up with stitches for the first time. It is really amazing that our injuries were not more serious. I am forever grateful that my car window was open, and that I was four-and-a- half years old, just small enough to fit through that window.

A few months later, we all walked down to Mom's friend's house. It was early fall, when the nights get cool after the sun goes down. I was five and in kindergarten, feeling all grown, and didn't want to wear a jacket, so I wore several layers of shirts to keep me warm. My brother and I joined a bunch of neighborhood kids playing hide and seek as the sun set.

I was hiding in between two houses when I felt something hot, sharp, and extremely painful on the back of my shoulder. I turned around and saw the figure of a much larger white man dart around the back of the house. I got a really bad feeling about this person, so I ran to the front of the house to warn the other kids. They told me that I was bleeding from my shoulder. That was when I realized that I had been stabbed.

My Mom and Dad took me to a hospital where I explained what happened. The Doctor took off my four layers of shirts and examined me. He took my parents aside and basically told them that if I say that I got stabbed, he would have to file a police report, which might end up with me in child protection. So, my parents convinced me to tell the Doctor that I hadn't been stabbed; that I had actually fallen into a bush.

Having to tell that lie deeply wounded my spirit. It felt like I was being denied the most basic part of my sense of self, which was my truth; that I was being asked to violate my own self. I told the lie through gritted teeth and got stitched up. I still have a three-inch scar from that "bush" that penetrated my shoulder through four layers of clothing.

The lie meant that the man got away with hurting me, which just didn't seem fair to me or the people he might hurt after me. I was haunted by that lie for a very long time. Hide and Seek still creeps me out, triggering memories of that physical and emotional pain. I'm grateful that my wound was not more serious, and that he only stabbed me once.

As I look back, I understand that telling the truth would not have produced "fairness," which is what I felt was lacking in that moment. I couldn't have identified my attacker other than the fact that he was white, so the police couldn't have caught him; and who knows if they would have even believed me, instead suspecting one of my parents had hurt me, and I could have ended up being separated from my family for who knows how long. Maybe one of them could have ended up in jail. It felt so unfair at the time. It was the right call though, and I appreciate that Dr. for seeing the bigger picture.

The lesson: What is Right is very rarely what is Fair.

We took a family road trip to Indiana in the summer of 1960, a few weeks before my sixth birthday. There were two cars, so I believe my Mom's parents went with us too, since we were visiting Mom's relatives. We stopped at a gas station along the way, and my brother and I got out to use the drinking fountain in front of the building.

All of a sudden, my Dad came running towards us, yelling at us to stop. He seemed more scared than angry, and led us to another, nasty, fountain behind the building. As we headed back to the car, my Dad pointed out the "Whites Only" sign above the first fountain. I couldn't read yet, but he told me to always stay away from that sign. I had never noticed signs like that before, and I had never seen that kind of fear on my dad's face.

DAD, BRIAN, MOM, ME, NANNY, & BRO IN INDIANA

I heard the word "nigger" hurled at me several times on that trip. I didn't know exactly what it meant, but I could tell by the tone and the looks that accompanied the word that it didn't mean anything good. My Dad explained its meaning to me with tears in his eyes, and told me that I would hear this word many times in my life. He was right.

I felt scared and uneasy throughout the rest of that trip, and was very happy when we got back home, where I thought I would feel safer. But then I started recognizing that even though they didn't say the word, I saw that look from many white adults, even in my own neighborhood.

In February of 1960, four Black college students staged a sit-in at a Woolworth's lunch counter in Greensboro, North Carolina after they were refused service. Within a few weeks, sit-ins had spread across the country, making civil rights a crucial issue for the Presidential election of that year.

Dr. Martin Luther King, Jr. was arrested while leading a protest in Atlanta, Georgia. Presidential candidate John F. Kennedy Jr., along with his brother, Robert, intervened to secure Dr. King's release. John Kennedy had earned the public endorsement of Dr. King's father, thereby rallying the Black vote, helping to win the presidency for John F. Kennedy, Jr. He appointed his brother, Robert, to be the Attorney General and raised the expectations for equality for Black Americans.

That trip taught me that the best way to keep myself safe depended on my ability to protect white people's feelings above my own, and to present myself as "non-threatening" through my words, tone, and body language. Race was always in my face, but never EVER discussed. Every Black person knew though, that calling the cops was asking for trouble, and that if a white person called the cops on you, it would not end well for you. So you had to take whatever white people dished out. This is still true in 2020.

ME AT ABOUT 5 YEARS OLD

1st Grade

In the summer of 1960, three days after my sixth birthday, I was hospitalized with tuberculosis, a highly infectious bacterial disease, which I probably contracted a few weeks earlier during the trip to Indiana. That experience fundamentally affected me in ways that I'm still trying to understand.

I was placed in a children's ward, which was a huge room with beds all along the walls. I was the only Black kid, and it wasn't long until I realized that none of the other kids wanted to play with me. They didn't even want me to touch the things that they played with. I didn't understand at first, because up until then, I had always played with all kinds of kids on my block at home. We just saw each other as kids and played together.

But these kids treated me like I was somehow foul to be around. I couldn't understand why these kids saw me as some kind of ugly. I was very lonely for awhile, until I decided that those kids wouldn't be fun to play with anyway, and I questioned who was really the ugly one.

Every once in awhile it would be somebody's birthday, and they would get a cake and candles and presents from home. Only once was I offered a slice of cake, but I wasn't ever allowed to sit at the table with the kids for any meals. I took that slice of cake back to my bed and I savored every bite.

I thought about what I would do if I was still there long enough to get my own birthday cake. I just wouldn't have felt good about myself if I kept it all to myself. I would have given them each a slice because joy is so much deeper when it's shared.

This was the first time that I felt connected to the strength and resiliency of my ancestors.

I was told that I would be there for a few weeks. I was actually there for nine months. That's an incredibly long time when you're only six-years-old. In fact, another baby was born into my family while I was gone.

When you're six, you don't understand the concept of time. You don't know how to read a clock or a calendar. After awhile, you begin to wonder if anyone loves you, then, you begin to wonder if anyone even remembers you. Eventually, you stop crying and start to forget what your family looks like.

My parents had said that they would visit me frequently. I didn't see them for over seven months. Looking back, I understand that I had a communicable disease, so I wasn't just in the hospital, I was actually in quarantine. But, again, I was six. It felt like I had been abandoned and forgotten. Like I didn't matter anymore. I still struggle with that feeling, but I know that when it comes up now, it comes from that little girl within me, not from what is actually happening around me.

The nurses, doctors, even the janitors all wore masks, so every adult was anonymous to some degree. Each day was essentially the same: breakfast (best meal of the day), followed by medications (usually shots, and some nurses were less rough with their shots than others), followed by boredom until lunch, and then more boredom until dinner. The loneliness was bad, but the boredom was excruciating.

There was a TV attached to the wall on the ward. On Saturday mornings it was tuned to cartoons for us kids. During the week though, the nurses would watch soap operas and the news. Segregation was still very much alive in the South, and it took the Supreme Court ruling of 1954 to order that public schools be desegregated. Despite the ruling most Southern public schools continued to segregate.

On Nov. 14, 1960, I saw images of a 6 year-old Black girl named Ruby Bridges being escorted to her school in New Orleans by armed Federal troops. I watched as men with guns escorted this little girl who looked a lot like me through an angry white mob to walk into her school. She looked brave and strong, and I remember being so terrified at the level of anger and hate directed at her.

I was scared for her, and scared for me, too. If "they" could direct so much ugliness at this little girl, what would "they" do to me when I was unprotected? I wanted to hug her, and hold her hand, and not have her face that rage alone. I wanted to tell her that I see those same looks here in this hospital. It was traumatizing, and I had no one to talk to about it. I still carry some of that fear, even now. And I still don't understand why there was/is so much hate.

There was a bright spot during my quarantine. A couple of bright spots, actually. When September rolled around, I was allowed to go to the hospital school twice a week. In a very short time, I learned how to read, and I also developed a very special bond with my teacher, Miss Anderson.
Learning to read changed everything for me. It was the first time that I felt truly proud of myself. Reading not only gave me access to books, it gave me something to do, and sparked my imagination. I could escape the mundane dreariness of my reality, and completely immerse myself into fantasyland. Then, I learned how to tell time and read a calendar, so I was able to know when certain things usually happened. It gave some order to the daily routines. Reading also led to writing, so I could write letters to my family.

I loved school days, because I got to spend time with Miss Anderson. She treated me like I mattered to her; like she really saw me as a human being. Most days, there would be other kids in the class, but some heavenly days, I had her all to myself. We got through the day's lesson pretty quickly, and then we would just talk. She wanted to know about my family, and what I liked to do, and what I thought about. I felt like she truly cared about me, and I absolutely adored her. Those days alone with her were magical to me.

Towards the end of my quarantine, I had surgery to remove a lymph node. As the anesthesia wore off, I found myself in pain in a private room, with my Mom hovering over me. I heard, "Wake up or I'll give you a spanking," in her 'I really mean it' voice. I woke all the way up. Instead of being happy to see her, I wanted her to leave. I wasn't sure that I even wanted to go home anymore, but where else could I go? Where did I belong?

Coming home was painful and difficult for me in ways that I did not expect. I had spent all those months dreaming about the way that my family was when I left. But things weren't the same when I returned. Another baby was born a few weeks after I was hospitalized, so he was nearly nine months old when I returned. We had no knowledge of each other. My family had grown and changed in my absence, and I wasn't sure how to fit in. I felt like a stranger in my own home. In many ways, I was even lonelier at home than in the hospital in those first couple of weeks.

After I was discharged from the hospital, Miss Anderson wrote a letter to my mother convincing her that it was part of the teacher's job to check on my adjustment to home life. She came to visit me a few months later. We sat together on the porch and read and talked and laughed. It was glorious. I had never had moments like those with my own mother. I absolutely hated to see her leave without me.

Watching her drive away made me realize how badly I wished that she was my mother. She gave me everything that my mother didn't know how to. She promised to write to me, and I promised to write back. I never saw or heard from her again. I still get teary when I think about her.

For several months, I asked my mother if I had gotten a letter. One day she finally told me that I had gotten several, but she had thrown them all away. She wouldn't tell me why; just that I needed to "forget about that woman."

It devastated me that I couldn't reach out to Miss Anderson, and tell her how much she meant to me. I didn't want her to think that I had rejected her. I hoped that she could figure out that my mother was blocking our connection.

I must have made the mistake of speaking too highly of my relationship with Miss Anderson when I returned home. That relationship triggered some deep insecurity in my mother, and she cut off our communication. I don't think my Mom was jealous; I think she just wanted to use her power to deny my happiness. Decades later, I would discover that my

Grandmother had done the same thing to my Mom when she was a teenager, blocking communication with someone who was important to my Mom.

I now understand that my greatest strengths came from that quarantine experience. I learned to read in a few weeks, because I was extremely motivated to do so. I developed a huge imagination and I'm able to see a bigger picture than most other people. I see possibilities for solving problems. In fact, I see problems as opportunities for improvement. I like to figure out how to do things efficiently. I am calm in the face of adversity, and I'm willing to laugh at myself. I know that I am strong and I know how to survive. I am not afraid to be alone. I am empathetic, because I know what it feels like to be abandoned, ignored, and dismissed. That experience was the birthplace of my own resilience. It gave me the awareness to trust that I could survive hard things.

Shortly after my discharge, I had to return to regular school. My Mom took me up to get registered and meet with the 1st grade teacher, who did an assessment of my reading, writing, and math skills. She set a start date for me, and gave me an assignment. I was to make a report about Alan Shepard (same last name, different spelling), who was scheduled to be the first American in space on my first day of school. I had never written a report before, or knew what one looked like, and this was WAY before the internet. So, I had to go to the library and do research and read newspaper and magazine articles. I did it though.

I was already nervous about my first day of school, and nervous about the expectations for my report. The teacher called me up to the front of the room and introduced me to the class. Then she asked me to read my report to the class. She had not prepared me for that. Maybe it was better that way. I read my report, and then we watched Alan Shepard orbit the earth live on May 6, 1961. It was fascinating to me, and I forgot about my nerves. The stars and galaxies represent endless possibilities to me. A part of me still wants to be an astronaut.

As I settled into class over the next few days, I began to understand what my teacher was up to. Not one of the other kids knew how to read, so she was setting me up as a role model for them. She had me read books out loud to the class while she spent one-on-one time with kids who needed her attention. I enjoyed reading, so I didn't mind, and I wanted to be helpful. I also wanted my classmates to learn to love reading too. And it gave me a way to immediately fit in. A couple of those kids actually did learn to read, and it was so rewarding to see their faces light up when they figured it out!

Groups of white and Black American activists known as "Freedom Riders" rode buses throughout the South in 1961 to protest segregated bus terminals by trying to use "whites only" restrooms and lunch counters. The plan was to travel by Greyhound bus from Washington, DC, to New Orleans, LA. They encountered increasing violence along the way, eventually facing an angry white mob in Anniston, AL, where someone threw a bomb onto the bus. A second bus was also met with an angry mob in Birmingham, AL, where Freedom Riders were beaten and arrested.

These violent encounters were also getting publicity, gaining momentum for the Civil Rights movement.

hall. They usually went to their room shortly after dinner.

As I was reestablishing my relationship with my brothers, I would often sit on the floor in their room after we were sent to bed, and we would talk and try not to laugh too loudly, until my Dad would yell for us to go to sleep. Sometimes, he would come upstairs with the threat of a spanking. I had to listen carefully for the sound of his footsteps because if I got caught in their room, I would be in BIG trouble. I hid under the closest bed, and had to be very quiet when I snuck back to my room.

One night, I heard footsteps coming from the hall, not the stairs. It was my great-grandfather, and I was terrified. We all were. He stood in the doorway of my brothers' room for quite some time, and I could only see his silhouette from where I was hiding. He finally left, but I heard his footsteps stop in front of MY room. It seemed like he stood there forever. The thought of him going into my room filled me with dread. Eventually, he went back to his room, and I waited a good while before sneaking back to my bed.

I stopped spending time in my brothers' room after that, but I still remember my great-grandfather standing in my doorway several times in the following weeks. I was worried that he would sometimes be there when I actually was asleep. I became afraid to sleep. I started closing my bedroom door, so that he in 1961 to protest segregated bus terminals by trying to use "whites only" restrooms and lunch counters. The plan was to travel by Greyhound bus from Washington, DC, to New Orleans, LA. They encountered increasing violence along the way, eventually facing an angry white mob in Anniston, AL, where someone threw a bomb onto the bus. A second bus was also met with an angry mob in Birmingham, AL, where Freedom Riders were beaten and arrested.

These violent encounters were also getting publicity, gaining momentum for the Civil Rights movement.

2nd Grade

I don't remember my second grade teacher's face or name, but I remember that I dreaded being in her classroom. Even though there were more Black kids than white, she would rarely call on us Black kids, except when she knew that we were unlikely to know the answer, and then she would laugh out loud and ridicule us mercilessly for giving a wrong answer. I quit raising my hand in her classroom and hoped that she would never call my name. She did call on me once though, and I gave her the right answer. She gave me that look of anger and hate that I recognized, and she never called on me again. I spent a lot of time at recess consoling whoever had been her target for the day.

I had experienced racism before, but only from strangers. This teacher brought it directly to me. I expected her to have authority over me because she was a teacher, not because she was a white teacher. By treating all of the Black kids in her class with such disdain, she also taught the white kids to treat us that way too. She would claim that our turned-in papers were "missing," therefore making us do twice the work. Points were subtracted because these papers were now "late," so we could never get a decent grade. Despite her considerable efforts, I motivated myself to keep learning and to keep showing up. I often wonder how many Black minds she personally set up to accept that they were failures.

It was around this time that the black hole known as my Grandpa Tony came to live with us. Grandpa Tony was over six feet tall, loud, intimidating, and mean. He was actually my great-grandfather on my mother's side. He and his second wife, Grandma Lottie moved in with us for a few months. She was the complete opposite of him, kind, gracious, and generous of spirit. She was also a phenomenal cook, which my mother was not. We were all very grateful for Grandma Lottie's food!

Grandma Lottie was full of light and love. She brought a level of stability and nurturing to our home that was desperately needed. EVERYONE called her Grandma, including grown-ups. She was quiet and unassuming, but her smile was never far from her face. She had owned a restaurant in Georgetown, Kentucky, and that is where she met my great-grandfather. Even though she had never given birth to children of her own, she gave each of us her own kind of special motherly attention, something we had rarely experienced.

My parents slept in the bedroom at the bottom of the stairs. My three brothers had the room right at the top of the stairs, my room was down the hall, and my great-grandparents had the room at the far end of the hall. They usually went to their room shortly after dinner.

As I was reestablishing my relationship with my brothers, I would often sit on the floor in their room after we were sent to bed, and we would talk and try not to laugh too loudly, until my Dad would yell for us to go to sleep. Sometimes, he would come upstairs with the threat of a spanking. I had to listen carefully for the sound of his footsteps because if I got caught in their room, I would be in BIG trouble. I hid under the closest bed, and had to be very quiet when I snuck back to my room.

One night, I heard footsteps coming from the hall, not the stairs. It was my great-grandfather, and I was terrified. We all were. He stood in the doorway of my brothers' room for quite some time, and I could only see his silhouette from where I was hiding. He finally left, but I heard his footsteps stop in front of MY room. It seemed like he stood there forever. The thought of him going into my room filled me with dread. Eventually, he went back to his room, and I waited a good while before sneaking back to my bed.

I stopped spending time in my brothers' room after that, but I still remember my great-grandfather standing in my doorway several times in the following weeks. I was worried that he would sometimes be there when I actually was asleep. I became afraid to sleep. I started closing my bedroom door, so that he would have to open it to see me and I would at least know when he was there. After being in quarantine in a ward full of children for so long, it was scary for me to sleep in the closed room, but seeing his shadow in the doorway was even scarier. There may be more that I'm not remembering, and that deeply concerns me. After a few months, they moved in with another relative, which was a huge relief for me. I don't remember why they moved.

The sibling closest to me in age was almost exactly two years younger than me. I called him "Bro," because I couldn't say the word brother at the time he was born. It was a name that just stuck. He was my very first friend in life. We spent a lot of time together when we were little, and I cherish his friendship to this day.
When Bro was old enough, we would walk the four blocks back and forth to school together. There was no school lunch then, so we came home for lunch everyday. At some point during his first year at school, a girl my age started bullying him on our way home. I told her to stop, but each day it got worse, and she got more aggressive. One day, she actually pushed him from behind, and I had had enough.

I turned around and pushed her away. She came at me, and I let her take a swing at me, because I was just too mad to be scared. I easily dodged her swing and pushed her hard enough to make her fall. I was ready to punch her if she came at me again, but she stayed on the ground. I leaned over her and told her to never come near us again. No one bothered either one of us after that.

Over the years I had at least one "exchange" like this on behalf of each one of my siblings. I am incredibly uncomfortable with confrontation on my own behalf, but I will "go there" to protect someone else.

My parents bowled in a Black league on Friday nights, so Bro and I had unsupervised free rein of the common areas at the bowling alley. We played tag, Simon Says, racing, and just running around with the other unsupervised kids. Every once in awhile, one of us would catch the angry attention of a grown-up, and get hauled off by our parent for a spanking. It was a good time, in general. After bowling...not so much.

There was a Black-owned club called The Nacirema (American spelled backwards), and my parents were members. After bowling, many of the league members would meet up at the club for drinks. My parents would leave me and my three brothers, the youngest in a cloth diaper (no disposables in 1961), sitting in the car. They said they would "make it quick," but it always ended up being several hours. We had no food or water while we were waiting, and no access to a bathroom. I would have to change wet/stinky diapers in the car. My other brothers could pee in a bush somewhere, but I would just have to hold on.

One time, I just couldn't wait any longer, so I had to flag down a person that I recognized as they were going inside and ask them to get my mother. She wasn't happy, but she took me inside the club to use the bathroom. I had always been curious about what went on in there. It was loud and smoky and crowded. There was music coming from the stage and lots of laughter. It smelled really good, once my nose got past the cigarette smoke. She told me to hurry up, because I was not supposed to be in there, and I did.

They were both drunk when we would finally go home. I would pretend to be asleep because I was too furious to talk, and Dad would carry me upstairs to my room and tuck me in. We repeated this routine for many Fridays over that summer and fall. As fall turned to winter, my uncle or grandmother would babysit us at home on Fridays, which was better, at least when "Uncle Funny" (my mother's only sibling, Freddie) came over. He actually WAS fun and played games with us, and didn't yell at us for being too loud. He let us stay up way past our bedtime. As the night wore on, he would be on the lookout for my parent's return, and give us a heads-up, so we could scramble to our rooms and pretend to be asleep.

3rd Grade

One summer day when I was 8 years old, a neighborhood kid's bike went missing. My brothers and I spent some time helping to look for the bike, until I was summoned home by my Dad. He took me to my room, and accused me of taking the bike. I was completely confused. I told him that I didn't take the bike, and didn't know where it was. He didn't believe me. He gave me a spanking, and told me to stay in my room until I was ready to say where the bike was.

A few hours later, the bike was found, and the real thief was uncovered. My Mom came into my room to tell me that my Dad was sorry for not believing me. The fact that he didn't say it to me himself broke my heart more than the actual spanking did. I lost some respect for him, and it took me a long time to feel like I could trust him again.

When my second brother started kindergarten, I was in charge of making sure he got to school and home for lunch safely. One time, my little brother didn't meet us at our usual spot, so Bro and I went to his classroom. The teacher told us that everyone had left. We looked all over the school and couldn't find him. We looked everywhere again, mostly to avoid facing Mom's wrath. We were full of dread walking home.

Mom was furious when we walked in, and there was our little brother, at the kitchen table, finishing his lunch with a big smile. He had been released a few minutes early, and walked home by himself. So now Bro and I were in trouble for being late, and we no longer had enough time to eat lunch. We got spanked before dinner. It took a long time to forgive my little brother for that one.

In 3rd grade, I had a teacher that I loved and respected, Mrs. Williams. She was the first Black teacher that I had ever seen, and the only Black teacher I would have until high school. Mrs. Williams was big and loud, but she was also fair. She spread her attention around the room, and made us all feel seen and valued.

Every Friday afternoon, she would hold a spelling bee in the class, and the winner received fifty cents, which was a lot of money back then. Our school was across the street from an ice cream cone shop, a concept that would later become Dairy Queen. Thanks to my love of reading, no one could beat me. I won that spelling bee every week.

Mrs. Williams asked me to stay after class one day. She asked me how winning the bees made me feel and she told me that I needed to lose the next bee. She said that I needed to give someone else a chance to win so that they could experience the feeling that I did. She said she would still give me the money because she knew that it would be hard for me to lose on purpose, and she was right.

Growing up with only brothers made me extremely competitive; losing on purpose was not in my nature, but I loved her and trusted her. I tried to put myself in the other kids' shoes, and I understood what she was saying. It was incredibly hard, but I threw the next competition, and a few weeks later, I asked her to just let me run the competition. I realized that winning the spelling bee just wasn't fun for me anymore, and it was more fun trying to guess who WOULD win. She agreed, and the rest of the class started getting excited about having an actual chance to win. It was an important lesson, because I still have that competitive nature and always want to be first, but I try to give others an opportunity to shine, too.

No one had ever rooted for me to win, and I didn't understand why. I was so caught up in the competition that I couldn't see that I was also crushing everyone else's spirit. They didn't like me, and they didn't like the spelling bee. Mrs. Williams taught me that winning isn't always about being first. There is so much more to learn about ourselves when we take a back seat sometimes.

In the summer of 1963, Governor George Wallace of Alabama stood in the doorway of the University of Alabama to block Black students from registering to attend classes. He continued this stance until President John F. Kennedy sent in Federal Troops. Wallace believed wholeheartedly in "segregation now, segregation tomorrow, segregation forever," and served as Alabama's Governor for four terms, which means he had a LOT of support. He also ran for President of the United States, which truly frightened me.

Also in June of 1963, President Kennedy introduced Civil Rights legislation to Congress. Many states in the South were still segregated and openly restricted Black people from voting. There was a lot of pushback to the legislation proposed by President Kennedy.

In August of 1963, 250,000 people took part in the March on Washington for Jobs and Freedom. They heard Dr. Martin Luther King, Jr. deliver his "I Have a Dream" speech as the closing address in front of the Lincoln Memorial.

4th Grade

We moved to a different neighborhood and school in the summer between 3rd and 4th grade. The house was a little bigger, the backyard was much better, and the garage was attached, which seemed really cool to me at that time. The walk to school was shorter, and there was a park nearby, which we all spent a great deal of time at. Another baby brother was born. My great-grandparents moved back in with us so that my mom could go to work.

Grandma Lottie and I would catch a bus to go grocery shopping every couple of weeks or so. I would tell her about school and ask questions about life in Kentucky. We always bought a frozen coconut cream pie to enjoy later. No one else in the house liked coconut, so it was our special treat. We brought our groceries home on the bus and put them away as we waited for our coconut cream pie to thaw. We would sit at the table with a knife and two spoons, watching the clock for the one hour thaw. She cut the pie into eight slices, and we sat together enjoying our coconut cream pie for four straight nights. It was glorious, because I got to have her attention all to myself during those magical times.

GRANDMA LOTTIE

She was an amazing cook, and she taught me a few of her secrets. I really miss her apple pie, which she made from scratch, including the crust.
Every year though, usually in the early fall, she would make "chitlins" which is basically pig intestines, cleaned and then boiled for several hours. The smell was horrific, and carried for several blocks. In fact, the smell would permeate our entire school whenever someone nearby would cook them.

A bunch of us neighborhood kids would walk home together after school, and as we got closer to our homes, we could all detect that odor. We would look at each other with pity and dread as we got closer to identifying the source. Kids would peel off of our group with great relief when they realized the smell was not coming from the direction of their house. Our eyes would be watering by the time we reached our front door, having figured out that the smell was coming from OUR house, and we prayed internally for an alternative choice for dinner. Thankfully, there usually was.

Chitlins as a meal comes from the days of slavery. On butchering day, the masters would get the best cuts of meat, and the slaves would get what was left; pig ears, snouts, feet, and intestines for example. These were considered to be delicacies by the slaves. Not every day was butchering day, so most meals were far less substantial. These foods are still part of what is called "soul food."

Grandma Lottie couldn't read or write, so whenever she got a letter from a relative I would read it to her, and she would then dictate a response. Every December 1st, she would pull out her box of letters and cards and addresses so that I could write her Christmas cards. I would write what she told me to. I learned a lot about her that way. She didn't know how to sign her name, so she would put an "X" and I would write her name below. I loved her dearly.

Grandpa Tony, on the other hand, made mealtimes unbearable for me. He mocked the way that I ate, the way that I spoke, and everything that I did. He bullied me constantly, and none of my brothers came to my defense. They were just relieved that they weren't his target, and didn't want to draw his attention.

He called me "Pimples on your tongue" instead of calling me by my name. I had no idea that everyone has tastebuds. I only knew that I did, in fact, have bumps on my tongue, so I felt like there was something horribly wrong with me. I stopped talking around him, and then I stopped talking in general. I didn't know it then, but that was his goal for me.

He would often be standing outside the bathroom door when I emerged, and he would say, "I know what you were doing in there." He implied that whatever I had been doing was somehow dirty and disgusting and just not normal. I began to isolate myself and withdrew from my family.

Eventually, I would come home from school, and go immediately to sleep in my parent's bed. I'd wake up when my parents got home from work late at night, eat the dinner that Grandma Lottie had set aside for me, and do the dishes and my homework while everyone else was asleep. I'd watch movies on TV, mostly musicals or Charlie Chan until morning. I did all of that for several months to avoid being around my great-grandfather. No one ever asked me about it.

I once overheard someone describing me as "shy." I had never thought of myself in that way before. I was observant, maybe quiet, but that word "shy" really threw me. and I thought that might actually be what was "wrong" with me. I don't think it changed my external behavior, but that word rattled around in my head for decades. It became a way that I described myself TO myself, but it was also something that I struggled to actually BE. I eventually realized that I had allowed my great-grandfather to stifle my voice. I burned through decades of time, energy, and inner turmoil trying to become someone else's judgement of who I actually was. I finally realized that only I can decide who I am. I don't think of myself as shy anymore.

In September of 1963, a bomb went off at the 16th St. Baptist church in Birmingham, AL, killing four young Black girls, and injuring many others. The FBI concluded in 1965 that the bomb was planted by four Ku Klux Klan members No one is prosecuted until 1977, when one of the Klan members was found guilty of the murder of only one of the little girls. Two other Klansmen were convicted in 2001 and 2002. The fourth Klansman died before being convicted.

I was in 4th grade when President John F. Kennedy was assassinated. This was my first exposure to tragedy, and it felt like it affected the entire world. I believed that JFK was somewhat sympathetic to the Civil Rights movement. Segregation was still very much alive in the

South and the Ku Klux Klan continued to terrorize Black communities that were trying to exercise their right to vote by burning crosses and lynching Black men. JFK seemed willing to at least entertain the concept of equality. And then he was murdered in broad daylight.

When you're nine-years-old and see your young and vibrant President get shot in the head, it is truly traumatizing. I think I was in shock for at least a week. I was scared about what his death meant for our country, and what it meant for Black people. It was hard for me to imagine that the world wouldn't turn upside down, that the Klan would now be free to ride into my neighborhood and burn my house down. It was hard to sleep because the Klan rode at night, and I was afraid they would try to drag my father away and hang him from a tree.

The world moves on in the face of tragedy, though. Vice President Lyndon Johnson assumed the Presidency, and the Civil Rights movement continued. The bombing of the church and the spirit of continuing the legacy of President Kennedy contributed to increasing support for the movement. President Johnson signed the Civil Rights Act of 1964 into law, preventing discrimination in employment, education, housing, and transportation due to race, color, sex, religion, or national origin. It didn't end segregation, it was just no longer legal to do so.

Dr. King became the youngest person to receive the Nobel Peace Prize, delivering one of his most powerful and often quoted speeches. I completely believed in his vision of truth, justice and equality. He was a hero to me, and demonstrated strength and resiliency in its finest form.

5th Grade

Finally! A sister! Grandma Lottie and I both adored her. She was born with a rare disorder, hyperlipidemia, meaning her body was unable to properly process fat. At the time of her diagnosis, only about a dozen people in the world had been diagnosed, so there wasn't much knowledge on how to treat her. She spent much of her childhood in and out of hospitals. We were told that she wouldn't live past the age of ten. They were wrong. She is very much alive decades later, and I still adore her.

I came home from school one day when I was ten-years-old to find my Mom waiting for me, which was not normal. She said that she and I were going to catch a bus. She wouldn't tell me where we were going, and she did not seem happy. I always had this fear that I would be taken back to the hospital, so I was scared. We got off of the bus downtown, went into Dayton's department store, and made our way to the lingerie department.

ME, SAMANTHA, BRIAN, BRO, BILLY, & DAVID

A lady asked if she could help us, and my Mom pushed me towards her and said, "She needs a bra," like I was guilty of something, and then Mom turned and walked away. It was awkward and embarrassing for the saleslady and me, but the lady was very nice to me, and educated me about fit and function. My mom and I didn't talk at all on the way home, even though I had so many questions.

A few weeks later, I noticed that there was blood every time I used the bathroom. In fact, what started out as spots turned into a constant flow. I had no idea what was happening, and had no idea how to stop it. I kissed my brothers goodbye, crawled into bed, and waited to die. I wasn't scared about it, just very sad.

Another relative stopped by and asked me what was going on. I told him that I was dying, and to tell everyone that I loved them. He figured out what was really going on, and he told me that I wasn't going to die. I could hear him talking angrily on the phone with my mother. He told her to get her butt home right now and talk to her daughter.

She was clearly uncomfortable and didn't really tell me much. She just gave me some "equipment," and said she was getting me a book to learn about what was happening to my body. That was my introduction to menstruation. She made it clear that she did not want to talk about it with me, and we never did, but she asked a slightly older girl in the neighborhood to talk to me. I barely knew this girl, and she was just as confused about why we were having this conversation as I was.

When my sisters got to the appropriate age, Mom asked me to talk to them about growing up and their changing bodies. I was ok with doing that for my sisters' sake, because I wanted them to be better prepared than I was. I wanted them to feel safe, not completely exposed. I didn't want them to have to talk to strangers about such intimate things, like I'd had to do.

Even though my body was moving into womanhood, I fully embraced my tomboyishness, and during the summer months I was outside playing games with my brothers and their friends all the time. Because I was a girl, I had to prove that I belonged in their club. I was pretty good at sports, but I was still "a girl," so my goal was to be so good that I wouldn't be last when it came time for the boys to pick teams. Once, I got picked in the second round, and I was extremely proud of that. No one would cover me when we played football, so I was always open, but they would rarely throw me the ball. When they did, though, I always tried to catch it, because it was an easy touchdown since no one was covering me.

We played all kinds of games; kickball, softball, football, tag, hide and seek, kick the can, and we would often walk or bike to the park to play on the playground, "swim" in the pool (it was only three feet high), play softball, basketball, baseball, volleyball and tetherball. The girls in the neighborhood would want to play hopscotch and jump rope, and those games were ok, but only when it was your turn, in my opinion. There was a lot of downtime when it wasn't, so those games weren't priority for me.

Back then, most girls weren't particularly active, in fact they were encouraged to be INACTIVE with dolls and play kitchens and houses. I never understood the value of pretending that a doll had a better and more active life. When someone asked what I did today, I was expected to say "Well, Barbie and Ken went to the beach in their fancy red car." How boring is that? I preferred to be moving, and since the other girls didn't want to do that, I had to hang with the boys. Girls didn't like me because I hung with the guys, and moved my body differently than the girls did. I often had scrapes and bruises, but I wasn't afraid of getting hurt, like most girls were. My legs are long and lean because of all of that childhood activity, and are still my favorite feature.

I developed a serious love for tetherball, and I was the queen of the court for several years. I would be on the court for hours, because hardly anyone could beat me. Tetherball has a rhythm that I felt in my bones. I knew how to play defense to set up my offense. I played against everybody, so I knew what their strengths and weaknesses were, and I adapted my game accordingly. Most of my opponents would just try to hit the ball harder, not smarter. For me, it wasn't just about the ball; it was also about where the opponent was standing in relation to the ball and on the court. From there, it's all about angles and understanding that the ball moves faster as the rope wraps around the pole. Boom! Next!

We didn't have money for elaborate vacations, but once or twice each summer, we would spend about a week at a family friend's cabin up north. It was very rustic, and not really big enough for all of us. When we first started going, there was only an outhouse for a bathroom. It was really scary to use during the day; at night, it was absolutely horrifying. The boys, of course, could pee wherever, but my Mom and I had to use the outhouse every time. My Mom was terrified of spiders, so not only did she make me go with her, she also made me go in first to make sure no spiders were inside. If there were, I had to kill them to protect her. I trained myself to take care of my own business during daylight hours. Over the years, the cabin was renovated to expand the living space and include a much appreciated indoor bathroom.

On one trip to the cabin, we stopped at a restaurant to have breakfast. We were the only ones there as I recall. Us kids wanted pancakes, and Mom and Dad had bacon and eggs. The pancakes weren't great, but we were hungry, and ate them all. Ten minutes after leaving the restaurant, all of us kids had serious stomach issues, all at the same time. Fortunately, my Dad didn't question our distress, and stopped at the first rest stop. I was old enough to understand that this was no coincidence. There was something funky in those pancakes. I also understood that even though he wanted to, Dad could not confront those people at the restaurant. They wouldn't have admitted to sabotaging our food, and he couldn't prove that they did. That was a tough lesson, and I still feel vulnerable every time that I dine out.

My favorite part about being up at the cabin was going fishing in the boat with my Dad. I actually didn't enjoy the fishing, I just liked being with him on the peaceful water. He was very patient with us, and rarely fished himself, because we kept him busy baiting our hooks. When I realized that he wasn't fishing, I asked him to show me how to bait the hooks, and I took some of that burden off of him. Plus, I wanted him to be proud of me. I think he was. I'm not much of an outdoors person, but I have very fond memories of those trips to the cabin.

MY DAD

We were kids, so sometimes we would get into trouble. Mom's spankings were no joke. She would send us outside to get a branch from a tree, and if that branch didn't meet her approval, she'd pick one herself, and it would be about twice as thick as our choice had been. We all learned that lesson the hard way. Once a branch was selected and approved, it had to be stripped of bark, which also gave us time to re-evaluate our life choices, and steel ourselves for the pain that was heading our way. It was a period of absolute dread. Meanwhile, she was watching us strip the bark, allowing her time to reflect on our transgression as well, and build up her anger. Some of us tried to delay the inevitable by slowing down the stripping process, but that only fueled her rage even more. Stripping the bark made the branch more flexible and whip-like. It also made the branch slightly damp. None of that was good.

She would grab one of our arms, and start swinging. The first whack to our bare-skinned behinds was shocking; by the third whip, the pain was excruciating, and natural instincts took over. We tried to escape the pain by running, but she had a firm grip, so we could only run in a circle. She would swing harder to make up the distance, so we would use our free arm to try to protect our bare butts. That enraged her, and she would keep swinging until we surrendered by dropping our protective arm and letting her have unobstructed whacks. It was horrific.

MY MOM

The worst part was her betrayal when our Dad came home from work. She would tell him what we had done, but not what she had already done to punish us. So, he would spank us again. He, at least, would give us the choice of his belt or his hand, and we always kept our pants on. We would have to lay across his lap so that he could use his free hand and upper body to keep us from squirming too much and trying to cover our backsides.

Eventually, he caught on to the fact that we had already paid a steep price for our transgressions. I think he may have inadvertently seen some welts that mom had left on one of us. So he started taking us to the attached garage for our spankings, and if he felt that the punishment didn't fit the crime, he would smack something else, and we would yelp as though we were actually getting spanked. The tears I shed were about feeling protected; a feeling that I still don't experience very often.

One time, my mom sent my brothers to take out the trash. In those days, we all burned our own trash in steel containers. She specifically told them to NOT start the fire. They seemed to be gone longer than necessary, so she looked out the back window, and then she quietly went outside. I could see my brothers had not only started the fire, they were looking around the yard for other things to throw into the fire, laughing and having fun.

Meanwhile, my mom was pulling branches from the tree in our backyard, and stripping them herself. I knew my brothers were gonna get it, but there was nothing I could do to save them. I tried waving my arms from the back door, but I couldn't call out to them because mom was there between us. All I could do was cry silently for them, while also rejoicing that I wasn't out there with them. The terror on their faces when they realized they were busted was absolutely real, and heartbreaking to witness.

I listened to the whippings and the weeping, and offered comfort to those willing to accept it. Not all were. I think the oldest of my brothers felt the most guilt and shame, even though starting the fire wasn't his idea, he didn't really try to stop it, and he was supposed to be in charge. It was a sad day for everybody. Except maybe my mom.

In March of 1965, the Civil Rights movement set out on a 54 mile non-violent march from Selma, AL to the state capitol in Montgomery to campaign for voting rights. On March 7, as the group, led by John Lewis, attempted to cross the Edmund Pettus bridge, they were met by a blockade of state troopers and local lawmen, who ordered the marchers to disperse. When they refused, the marchers were attacked with clubs and tear gas. Retreating marchers were chased by mounted police, continuing to beat them. This day became known as "Bloody Sunday."

The violent confrontations were televised, and awareness of the Movement grew. Resistance to the peaceful march was led by Alabama Governor George Wallace, who was ordered by a Federal Judge to abstain from harassing or threatening the Marchers. Federal troops were sent to protect the marchers as they continued to Montgomery.

On August 6, witnessed by Dr. King and other civil rights leaders, President Lyndon Johnson signed the Voting Rights Act, abolishing literacy tests and poll taxes designed to prevent Black people from voting.

6th Grade

I continued to do well in 4th, 5th, and 6th grade. My 6th grade teacher, Mr. Knoblauch, also played a significant role in my life. He made learning fun. None of us were happy whenever we had a substitute. Mr. Knoblauch let us have a talent show in class every other Friday. Me and two other girls would make costumes, create a dance routine, and lip sync to a Supremes song. A group of boys did the same thing to a Temptations song, although they usually didn't coordinate what they wore. We would often compete head-to-head for first place honors, determined by class vote. The only prize was bragging rights. Creating and performing was the ultimate prize just because it was so much fun.

Mr. Knoblauch convinced me to run for secretary of the student council. Girls weren't encouraged to run for president back then, and Black kids weren't encouraged to run at all. I won by promising to fight for longer recess time. Mr. Knoblauch told me that I had to now honor my campaign promise by having a meeting with the principal. He told me that I had to make a list of reasons why longer recess would benefit students and staff. I made my list and had my meeting. My proposal was denied, but the principal gave me props for my presentation, and I felt proud of myself for fulfilling that promise.

I was also a school patrol person, primarily because I wanted to go to the city-wide patrol picnic at the end of the year, which was a badge of honor and a celebration, also it was a day off of school. We spent the week before the picnic training in the 5th graders who would take over for the following year. Two days before the picnic, Mr. Knoblauch pulled me aside and asked me to skip the picnic to remain on duty to supervise the newbies. He said that I could think about it, but I knew that he was relying on me to make the responsible choice. That was an agonizing decision. I didn't like it AT ALL, but I decided to skip the picnic, take the responsibility, and let my heart break.

ME AND SOME BROTHERS (DAVID, BRO, & BRIAN)

It turned out that a huge fight broke out between rival schools over something ridiculously stupid, and the picnic was cut short. So, I wasn't alone in my disappointment that day.

That's the thing about being a leader. You often get asked to make painful choices that you don't get much credit for. Leadership isn't always about being at the front of the pack. It is often about sacrificing for the greater good.

The TV series Star Trek debuted in the fall of 1966, and featured a Black communications officer, Lieutenant Uhura, who was always visible and often utilized when the captain was on deck. This was a huge deal! I had never seen a Black woman portrayed as intelligent and vital, and her character helped me envision a future that included Black women as an integral part of society.

7th & 8th Grade

7th, 8th, and 9th grades were Junior High in my day. Again, there was no bussing; we all walked to school. The racial balance shifted dramatically to more white than Black, and the economic gap between white and Black became much more visible We had classes like Home Economics, where we learned to cook and sew, Auto Mechanics, Driver's Education, and Woodworking. These types of classes were elective, so we got to choose what we were interested in. They made school less boring, and we learned skills that we would actually use in life. I asked for, and received, a sewing machine for Christmas, and I made a lot of my own clothes in 8th and 9th grade.

Up until June of 1967, interracial marriage was illegal in about half of the states until the Supreme Court overturned that ruling in Loving v Virginia. Despite the ruling, some states were slow to change their laws. The last such state was Alabama, which finally changed their state constitution in 2000, thirty-three years after the Supreme Court ruling.

1968 had been filled with racial unrest, and Dr. Martin Luther King, Jr. led peaceful protests and marches throughout the south. These marches for Civil Rights usually ended in violence when the police would attack the protesters. The protesters would heal, and march again and again. Dr. King led a movement that was gaining strength across the country. People of all races were seeing the vicious assaults on TV. White people were finally witnessing the oppression of Black people, and public opinion was beginning to sway in favor of change. There was a genuine feeling of hopefulness in the Black community.

I was 14 years old in the spring of 1968 when Martin Luther King, Jr. was assassinated, shortly before a planned occupation of Washington, D.C. The shock, pain, and despair were overwhelming. The murder of Dr. King also killed momentum in the movement for Civil Rights. The light that Black people were heading toward was shattered with a single bullet. In the resulting darkness, rage grew, and the peaceful protests turned into riots that were met with military force. It felt like there was nowhere to be safe.

The riots resulting from anguish eventually became overshadowed as the race for the Presidency ramped up. So too did the protests over the Vietnam war. There was a military draft, meaning all males were assigned a number when they turned 18. Those numbers went into a lottery, and if your number was pulled, you were drafted into war. The Vietnam war had raged for years, thousands of soldiers died, and there seemed to be no purpose and therefore no clear end point. Protests started on college campuses and grew steadily across the country, erupting into a blood bath at the Democratic National Convention.

Shortly after winning the California primary, Presidential candidate and former U. S. Attorney General Robert F. Kennedy was assassinated. I actually watched this happen live on TV, as I was staying up all night to avoid being around my great-grandfather. It was shocking and horrific, and I was all alone. That scene is embedded in my memory.

On July 31, 1968, Charles Schulz introduced the first Black character, Franklin, to the Peanuts comic strip. He did so after many
months of back-and-forth letter writing with a Black woman, and he did it despite threats from his agent and newspaper publishers. I was thrilled to see Franklin's rare appearances, even though he was usually in the background.

9th Grade

We moved again in the summer between 8th and 9th grade when I was 14 years old, but we only moved a few blocks away, so we could all stay in the same schools. I got my own room, and my own record player. I was starting to feel more grown up. My great-grandparents moved along with us, which was blessing and a curse.

The house had four bedrooms and one-and-a-half bathrooms, which was half a bathroom more than we were used to for ten people. My Dad made a bedroom and a full bathroom in the basement, and that was where he and Mom spent most of their time.

The back yard was bigger than our previous home, and in the winter we would flood the yard and make an ice rink. Eventually, my Dad built a deck and installed a large screen house where he, Mom, and their neighborhood friends would drink beer together every evening watching baseball, basketball, or football, until winter came. Then they would all hang out in the basement.

There was a rule at my junior high school that girls could only wear dresses or skirts. No pants allowed. Winter in Minnesota is no joke, so girls would either leave their legs exposed to the elements, or change clothes when they got to school, which meant, carrying a dress and shoes along with the books, and getting to school early enough to change clothes in the girl's bathroom, which was wet and dirty from everyone's boots. I usually just wore pants under my dress, and left a pair of shoes in my locker. I could just slip my pants off right in front of my locker without exposing myself. Still, it was a pain.

A bunch of us girls started talking about it and decided to do something. We picked a day, and spread the word that every girl should wear pants to school that day. A lot of girls did. The principal made an announcement that any girl still wearing pants after second hour would be sent to the principal's office. Most girls changed clothes, but a handful, including myself, didn't. I hadn't even brought clothes to change into. I was prepared to be sent home.

About five or six of us were sent to the principal's office where we stated our case and stood our ground. It was decided that girls could wear pants on Fridays, and also if the outside temperature was below zero. By springtime, girls wore pants whenever they wanted, and it was never discussed again. I guess "they" decided that the world didn't end and boys didn't lose their minds if girls wore pants in school. I'm still very proud that I didn't cave on that day.

Rules can be changed if you're willing to stand up and take the heat. Many times, what benefits a smaller

GRANDPA TONY

group will also benefit the group at large. Be willing to compromise to get closer to your goal. If you can get your opponent to dip their toe into your pool of change, they will see that the change you are seeking is not as scary as they thought and be more willing to venture further in.

There was a church across the street from my school, and every Friday they held a dance for ninth graders. It cost $1 to get in. My family was barely getting by, so we didn't get allowance, but my Dad got paid on Fridays, so he would give me a dollar when he got home from work. I loved music and I loved dancing. In fact, I was voted "Best Female Dancer" for my class! I always looked forward to those dances.

One Friday, my dad called to say he was running late and wouldn't be home in time for my dance. He told me to borrow a dollar from my great- grandfather, and Dad would pay him back when he got home. I wasn't thinking about anything except the dance when I went to Grandpa Tony's room to borrow that dollar.

He pulled the bill from his wallet, and said I could have it if I gave him a kiss. I leaned in to kiss his cheek, and he grabbed the back of my neck, turned his head, and stuck his tongue in my mouth. As I pulled away, he grabbed my breast and said, "Does your boyfriend touch you like that?" I was shocked, horrified, and so angry. I snatched the dollar and ran all the way to the safety of the dance.

A few weeks later, I had to borrow a dollar from him again, but this time, I waited until a few minutes after Grandma Lottie had gone up to the room, trusting that her presence would provide safety for me. She was already in bed, with her back to the chair that he was sitting in. I kept my distance, and asked for the money. As I reached for it, he grabbed my wrist and shoved my hand in his crotch. I literally had the dollar, something I wanted, and his penis, something I didn't want, in my hand at the same time. It was horrifying. He said, "You like that, don't you?" I pulled away from him and left the room. My great-grandmother continued to "sleep."

The next time that my Dad was late, I just skipped the dance altogether, got the dollar directly from him when he got home, and saved it for the following week. It took me several weeks to gather the courage to tell my Mom what had happened. She said, "I believe you. Don't tell your Dad." And then she changed the subject, and we never talked about it again. I immediately understood that no one would protect me. I had to protect myself.

It took me decades to sort through the layers of damage those encounters caused. Obviously, there was a huge sexual abuse component. I realized that he had been grooming me all along. He had systematically silenced and isolated me with his bullying and intimidation for several years. I never blamed myself for what he did to me. That darkness and shame all belonged to him.

I did, however, feel completely abandoned by my mother and great-grandmother. They both chose to protect him over me. I didn't feel safe in my own home. I truly believe that my mother had also been abused by him. He would have been 23 years younger when she was my age, and therefore even stronger and more intimidating. I had several siblings, so I could easily avoid being alone with him. She only had a younger brother who I'm sure found other things to do when he was around, and perhaps she encouraged her brother to stay away to protect him.

Still, it makes me wonder how my mom could welcome such evil into her home, and leave her children so vulnerable without any warning. I think she somehow convinced herself that she was responsible for his actions, and that she was his only victim. Why continue to protect him after my revelation though? By not revealing her secret, she remained his victim and a slave to the shame that she accepted, for her entire life.

I'm pretty sure my grandmother had been abused by him as well, so this practice of sacrificing daughters was a generational pattern. My grandmother was an angry and bitter woman. She only laughed AT people, not with people. I never met her mother. I can only imagine the pain and suffering she had endured at my great-grandfather's hands.

It took me 50 years to connect those moments of abuse to the way that I feel about money. I always connected his abuse to sex and power, not to money. But I literally had both the dollar that I wanted, and what he wanted from me (his penis) in my hand. Of course it was connected to money! He made money dangerous for me, so I never felt comfortable with having it. I spent a ton of money on things I would never use. I'd buy pretty shoes, but I really don't go anywhere, so they weren't even worn. When I lost weight and cleaned out my closet, most of my shoes, and a lot of my clothes still had price tags on them. Never worn. That's when I understood that my relationship with money was deeply flawed.

Naturally, I moved out when I was 18, even though I could barely afford it. But as my sisters started to mature, I worried about what he would try to do to them, so I moved back home and rearranged my work schedule so that they would never be alone with him.

He had a stroke when he was in his 90's, and eventually ended up in a nursing home. They had to tie his wrists to his bed, because he either was trying to grab the nurses like he had grabbed me, or he was trying to pleasure himself. There was no more denying what he was really all about. He died alone, and I did not cry for him.

But I had to forgive him to free myself from the pain he inflicted.

So many lessons...
As I looked back, I can see that he was grooming me by silencing me. He was teaching me to distrust myself, and isolating me from the rest of the family. He knew exactly what he was doing all along, and I

almost fell into his trap.

There was never anything wrong with me.

ALWAYS trust my gut.

Secrets always come out, usually at someone else's expense.

Be very clear about who this secret actually protects.

Get professional help to deal with trauma.

Do not compare my trauma to someone else's. Some trauma is just more obvious.

It doesn't matter what happened to me as a child. I am still responsible for my own adult choices, as was he.

While I don't have more money, I have a better relationship with money, and am much more mindful of how I choose to spend both my time and my money.

I told my Dad about what my great-grandfather had done when my Dad was in the final weeks of his battle with lung cancer. He'd had no idea, and we wept together. I also told him that I believed my mother had been a victim of my great-grandfather as well, and my

Dad said that made a lot of sense and explained a lot about her.

My Dad did not have an easy life either. His father was violent, and my father was the oldest of two boys. He felt it was his duty to protect his mom and his brother, even though he was a child himself. He and his brother got called to the principal's office one day, where his mom and his grandmother were waiting. They took the boys from school and ran away, leaving the state to get away from my grandfather. They had no money, so they ended up in a navy port town, where his mom and grandmother serviced the sailors to earn money for the family.

My grandfather eventually remarried and started another family. I spent the night with my three cousins, all girls, in his home a couple of times, and his violent nature was still very evident. He became enraged at trivial things like an innocent comment, and beat the crap out of whoever caught his attention. I'm not talking about a spanking; I'm talking about fists, black eyes, and split lips. It was absolutely terrifying. I was too afraid to speak or to sleep.

After witnessing that, I would insist that the sleepovers be at my house. My cousins always appreciated being away from the constant threat of impending doom, although my grandfather rarely agreed to let them come over. He took too much pleasure in controlling his kingdom, and I think he feared what would be discussed in his absence, although it was never talked about.

SFC SHEPHERD (right)

When my father grew up, he served in the Army as a medical assistant in the Korean War. As the assistant, it was his job to go to the front line, treat and stabilize the wounded and prepare them for transport to medical facilities. He had no weapon, only medical supplies, so he was vulnerable, but that is how black soldiers were treated; always on the front line. He didn't talk much about his service beyond that. I'm sure he was haunted by what he saw and by the lack of support for his service. He was expendable, and he knew it.

When he was discharged, he returned home and started working for my great-uncle Eddie, my mom's uncle, at his car wash in Hopkins, MN. Cars were washed by hand in those days, and this business primarily prepared cars for dealer showrooms. They didn't just wash cars, they spray-painted engines and tires, and added custom detailing to car bodies. There was no concern for worker safety then, and no ventilation, except in the summer when they would leave the garage doors open. Every single person who worked there died of lung cancer, including my father.

My dad was the manager, so he was always the first one to arrive, and the last to leave. He also worked on Saturdays to earn extra money for the family. Sometimes, he'd bring us older kids with him to "help." Mostly I think, he brought us to get us out of Mom's hair. There was lots of room for us to run around and burn off energy, but our favorite part was the pop machine. The pop was bottled, beautiful colors, icy cold, and a rare treat for us. We scrambled to get our favorite flavor, but it all depended on what was stocked in the machine. Let's just say...feelings were hurt occasionally.

As my brothers grew into their teens, they were allowed to drive cars in and out of the garage. That privilege was never offered to me, even though I was older than all of them. They were also allowed to stay out later than I was, which was grossly unfair, and led to the beginning of my rebellious phase.

Ok, so I wasn't actually rebellious. I "ran away" from home once, for about 6 hours. But that was my version of rebellious...leaving the house without telling anyone where I was going. I'm not saying I was a perfect child, I just tried to be "good" and stay out of trouble, mostly just to avoid being spanked.

10th Grade

Grade school was more Black than white kids; Junior High was pretty much racially balanced, and the white kids were from our neighborhood, so in the same relative economic range. High school was entirely different. The white kids came from the big houses closer to the lake (meaning richer) and they were definitely in the majority. Most had never spent time with Black people before, and didn't want to now. The teachers were different too; mostly white and mostly male.

I got my permit to drive when I was 15, and I somehow convinced my Dad that I only needed a licensed driver with me in order to drive, not a licensed ADULT driver, so my licensed best friend and I were allowed to drive my Dad's car fairly regularly. I was a very careful driver because I was not a legal driver, so I stayed away from trouble. We mostly went shopping, to a movie, or grabbing fast food.

My parents played a lot of Jazz on their record player. I grew up listening to Ray Charles, Ella Fitzgerald, Dave Brubeck, Nat King Cole, Miles Davis, Sammy Davis, Jr., Louie Armstrong, and Johnny Mathis, among others.
As my own musical tastes began to develop, I gravitated to the Motown sounds of The Four Tops,

The Supremes, The Temptations, and Stevie Wonder to begin with. In my teens and 20s, I branched out to a variety of artists, including James Taylor, Chaka Khan, Earth, Wind, & Fire, Marvin Gaye, Hall & Oates, Jethro Tull, Average White Band, Blood, Sweat, & Tears, and Steely Dan.

My greatest musical love, by far, was (and still is) Chicago. That love would come full-circle for me 50 years later.

I got my first job when I was 15. I worked at Friar's Dinner Theater in downtown Minneapolis. I was a hostess, so I would greet people, take them to their tables, and give them a brief run-down of what they would experience. I also worked the box office, handling reservations, seating assignments, and ticketing. The best part of that job was watching the rehearsals for the next show run. I just loved watching the process of the show coming together.

The other good part of the job was payday. I loved buying things for myself, and making my own decisions. Of course, I bought clothes, but I also started purchasing albums. The first album I bought was Chicago Transit Authority. It was rock mixed with jazz mixed with a bit of classical. I had never heard anything like it before, and I absolutely loved it! I bought their next ten albums on the day they were released. This was LONG before computers and internet. I just established a relationship with the guys at the record store, and they would give me the heads-up.

When I first discovered Chicago, I made my closest brother, Bro, and his best friend, Sparky (aka bonus brother), listen to the album with me. I tried to get them to understand why I loved them so much. I wanted them to appreciate their music like I did. Sparky got it more than Bro, and he and I would talk about their music frequently.

Sparky went on to become a great sound engineer, and went on tour with top performers like Gloria Estefan and Stevie Wonder. Sparky called me in the summer of 2017 to say that he had been hired to be the sound engineer for Robert Lamm, lead singer/songwriter/founding member of Chicago! I was so happy and excited for him that I literally cried on the phone. A few months later, he brought me two Chicago t-shirts; one was autographed by Robert Lamm. I cried again.
I listened ONLY to Chicago for two solid years after Sparky got the gig. The theme for my 65th Birthday Party was Chicago. Sparky called to say that he was giving me two tickets to their next show in my area, so I invited my brother to come with me.

We hung out with Sparky for about an hour before the band arrived. Sparky introduced us to a lot of the crew, including the main sound engineer, who invited us to watch the show from the sound stage...best seats in the house! Sparky took us onstage so that we could see everything up close, and we took a picture in front of their instruments. We also got to see the playlist for the performance, which was really cool. Sparky had arranged for us to get his discount on merchandise, so I got two more t-shirts, and my brother bought a hat.

SPARKY, ME, & BRO ONSTAGE

ME & ROBERT LAMM

The show was absolutely incredible! I've seen Chicago perform before, but only from the nosebleed seats. The view that I had was exceptional! After the show, we got VIP treatment backstage. Sparky pulled me aside, and took me to meet Robert Lamm privately, in person! He was so sweet to me, and even kissed me on both cheeks! My brother and I got to take pictures with the entire band. It was a truly magical experience for me, from start to finish. It was such a full-circle moment from when I introduced Sparky to Chicago 50 years earlier.

I had always been a good student, not because of "learning," but because I was so competitive. I got mostly A's and a few B's and got called on frequently in class, until I hit high school and quit getting called on. And then there was Shakespeare and Algebra, languages that I just could not grasp. I failed my Shakespeare class and had to go to summer school to make up for it. The Algebra class completely changed the course of my entire life.

Another sister joined our family in the summer of 1969. I was fifteen years- old and over all of my Mom's pregnancies. When my Mother told me she was pregnant again, I said, "How could you do this to me? Do you realize that by the time this kid turns my age, I'll be 32?" I was completely ridiculous about it. My sister was born exactly one month before my sixteenth birthday, and I still consider her to be my greatest birthday gift.

11th Grade

We were about two weeks into our fall semester when the Algebra teacher announced that a new student would be joining our class. A few minutes later, I heard the door open, and as I turned to look, I felt as though I was moving in slow motion as I locked eyes with the boy that entered our class. Time slowed down to a crawl for me. It was an incredibly powerful feeling. His name was Jesse, and he had just returned from spending a couple of years in London where his Dad had been teaching psychology. He found a seat in the front row, while I tried to figure out what had just happened to me. And, yeah, I thought he was cute.

After class, he hung out in the hallway with a few people that I knew casually, so I hung out there too. Within a few days, it became clear to me that another girl liked him, so I had to get there first (competitive). I had never had a boyfriend, so I had no idea how things "worked," but one day after class, I asked him to walk me home from school. He said Ok, and we agreed on a place to meet. I was so nervous and excited to see him waiting for me after school.

We got off to an awkward start, at least for me, because he didn't offer to carry my books, which is what guys did in the movies and on TV, so I thrust them into his chest and he carried them the rest of the way. He talked a LOT, which was OK, because other than thinking he was cute, I didn't know much about him.

He told me about his parents and his two younger brothers. He told me about spending the last two years in London, and sailing on a cruise ship there and back. I had only been to Indiana once by car, so his stories were fascinating to me.

I hadn't really thought about what would happen when we got to my house, so I invited him in to meet whatever siblings were around, and Grandma Lottie. They all greeted each other and I walked him to the door. He asked if he could kiss me, and I said OK (having never been kissed by a boy before), and he kissed me quite passionately, and then he left.

There is more to tell, but I don't think my kids would appreciate knowing those parts, so I'll just say that we were "together" for about three weeks until I broke up with him. He wanted to move WAY faster than I did, and I just wasn't ready. He moved on quickly, and we remained friends, even after high school. We started dating in 1983, got married in 1991, raised five children, and were together until he passed away on Thanksgiving Day, 2016.

High school was rough, but I did find pleasure in being on the Varsity volleyball team. I loved that game so much! I was really good at anticipating where the ball was going, and I had no fear of diving to save the ball. I was also good at controlling my bump, so I was a solid defensive player. I never mastered the overhead serve, but I had a wicked underhand serve that always scored several points by itself. I was so proud when I received my "W" for Washburn High School.

Even though I never learned how to read music, I also loved being in the choir, despite being the only Black person. I was an alto, and listened to the other altos to learn my part. What I enjoyed the most though, was some of the friendships that developed in choir and lasted throughout our lives. My best friend in high school and choir was Tim Turner. He had an amazing, beautiful tenor voice! We laughed so much together. He was just fun and silly and awesome.
Every other year, the choir would travel somewhere in the world to take part in a choir competition, and our choir was scheduled to compete in London. My family was not rich, but the choir raised money to bring the collective cost down, and between the money I made from my job at the dinner theater and with the help of my parents, I was able to make the trip.

A few days before departure, the choir director pulled me aside and told me I needed to "fix" my hair for the trip. I had a lot of hair back then, and it would take me two hours to wash it, comb through it, put about 30 rollers in it, and let it dry overnight. The next morning, I would get up early, take out the rollers, and divide each roll into about ten little curls. It took forever, but I felt pretty when it was done. The style would last about three days before the curls lost their definition from either humidity or sleeping on them. I would pick out the curls and wear an afro until the next wash day. I made my hair look pretty on the day of the trip.

I had never even been on a plane before, and here I was, flying across the ocean! Tim knew how much this trip meant to me, and he somehow managed to get people to change seats so that I could sit by a window and he could sit next to me. It was glorious! He took good care of me and included me in his group of friends (who eventually became my friends too), so that I was never left out and lonely.

We landed in London and stayed at a college dorm for the competition. I got to see Big Ben, and ride a double-decker bus, and shop at FAO Schwartz, and so many other things I had only seen in movies. It was an incredible experience for me, and opened my eyes to a bigger world.

We spent three nights in London, singing twice in the competition, and then we travelled by train to Paris, which was so grand and beautiful. I saw Notre Dame and the Avenue des Champs-Élysées, and took the elevator inside the Eiffel Tower at night, which was breathtakingly gorgeous. We sang in an absolutely stunning cathedral, and I will always remember the sound of our voices echoing throughout the chamber.

From Paris, we travelled by boat to a small city in Belgium. We were broken into pairs and stayed with families in town for our last two nights of the trip. There was a language barrier, plus the awkwardness of being in a stranger's home, but they treated me well. A group of us went to a club one evening to dance and have fun. The DJ kept playing the Rolling Stones "Brown Sugar," which was clearly meant for me. I didn't see a single Black person during my time in Belgium. The food got progressively worse for me as the trip went on, but I did my best. All in all, it was an incredible experience that I have carried in my heart since 1971.

And my hair soaked up the London humidity and went afro almost immediately. Everyone survived.

12th Grade

Our Senior Class play was "Don Quixote," which had always been my favorite play by far at the dinner theater where I worked. I knew every line by heart, and I auditioned for the lead female role of Dulcinea. No one else knew that story like I did, and I thought that my audition went well. I was cast as a background prisoner with no lines. It was disappointing, but I was still excited to be a part of it. Thanks to my connections with the dinner theater, I was able to secure the huge staircase which was crucial to the play.

We performed on stage for three nights, and on the third night, one of the other extras didn't say his two-word line. There was an awkward pause while we waited, and I just said the line, and the play moved on.

My Mom came to the final performance. I saw her walk in. She was the last to arrive, sat in the last row by the door, and was the first to leave. I can't tell you how many performances and volleyball games I participated in and would scan the crowd looking for my parents. That was the first time someone had shown up for me. It was bittersweet. I was glad that she had been there, but disappointed that she didn't stick around so that we could share a moment together. As a result though, I always tried to be there for my own kids, and witness their delight when they

HIGH SCHOOL GRADUATION

spotted me. I also saw many of the other kids scanning the crowd, and recognized their heartbreak when they accepted the fact that no one was there for them. I tried to boost those kids as well after the performance to let them know that they had been noticed and were being celebrated.

I basically coasted through my last year of high school. My parents had never discussed the possibility of college for me, so I didn't even consider it for myself. The only future I really saw was graduating, getting a full-time job, and moving out on my own. I moved in and out of my parents' home at least a half-dozen times over the following sixteen years as my life descended into alcoholism. I have tapped into my inherited and earned resiliency many times, and have remained sober since 1988.

I started paying more attention to politics, and voted in every general election and most primaries after I became eligible to vote. I remain grateful to have the honor and privilege of voting, and encourage everyone to exercise their right and responsibility to vote.

It took lots of blood, sweat, tears, hard work, and the support of powerful allies to make advancements toward "liberty and justice for all" during the Civil Rights Movement. As of this writing in 2020, there is still a very long way to go.

Efforts are still underway to make it difficult for Black people to vote. Black people still largely live in segregated sections of cities with little access to green space, fresh food, and transportation. Because public school resources are tied to property taxes, the poor sections of cities lack access to quality primary education, which leads to limited qualifications for higher education and therefore limited access to higher paying jobs.

Since the inception of slavery, the jobs that Black people do are considered "essential," but are not compensated much beyond minimum wage. Our country has the means and the willingness to continue to build jails when that money could be better used to build quality education in poor neighborhoods, and fair compensation for meaningful employment.

Even now, in 2020, Alabama's state constitution still bans mixed-race marriage, mandates school segregation, and allows poll taxes, meaning it is legal to have to pay to vote, although most of these laws are no longer enforced. Still, efforts to amend the language in the constitution have been defeated twice in the last decade. Overwhelming support for overt and systemic racism through including this language in the state constitution continues.

There are plenty of examples of racist language that still exist in many state constitutions across this country. Here is one: The bill of rights in the 1857 Minnesota Constitution says "there shall be neither slavery nor involuntary servitude in the state otherwise than as punishment for a crime of which the party has been convicted."

As of 2020, the Minnesota Senate majority leader, a Republican, says that he is "willing to take a look at" changing that language.

Ripple Effects

I spent several months in the beginning of 2019 struggling to understand why I was so distracted and unable to focus, why I couldn't sleep, why I could barely make myself take a shower. I thought I might be depressed, so I sought therapy, and I was diagnosed with Persistent Depression. I attended therapy and took my medications regularly, and thought I was handling my shit. And then, I got hit with a severe episode of PTSD (post- traumatic stress disorder) on Jan 1, 2020. I felt it throughout my entire body, as if I had walked into a wall.

I never would have defined my more dramatic experiences, flying through a car window, being quarantined at age 6, getting stabbed in the back, my Mother's indifference, and my great-grandfather's abuse, as traumatic. I always felt as though that word was reserved for life-threatening situations; you know, like military vets and victims of rape and assault. I didn't believe I should claim that word for myself.

But when I look at the definition of trauma: a deeply distressing or disturbing experience; or as in Wikipedia: Psychological trauma is damage to the mind that occurs as a result of a distressing event. Trauma is often the result of an overwhelming amount of stress that exceeds one's ability to cope, or integrate the emotions involved with that experience. When I look at my experiences through that filter, then hell YEAH I've been traumatized.

Understanding how I coped with those traumas helps me also understand what triggers those coping mechanisms. I can now see that my flight/fight or avoidance behaviors, which have become deeply ingrained habits, no longer serve me. They actually prevent me from developing the close connections that I sincerely desire. I'm discovering that I have to especially love these flawed parts of myself in order to access the love that I want to give to others.

The last line of the United States Pledge of Allegiance says "with liberty and justice for all." The most basic and fundamental element of freedom is the right to vote, meaning it should be easily accessible for everyone, especially in the midst of a pandemic. And yet, even in 2020 there have been massive efforts to make voting in this presidential election extremely difficult, including deliberate slow down of the Postal Service so that mail-in votes won't be received in time to count. There are even lawsuits aimed at throwing out votes cast in certain ways.

In Minnesota, for example, absentee ballots have always had to be postmarked by election day, meaning they would arrive a few days after election day, but they would still be counted. This year, FIVE DAYS before election day, a federal court ruled that ballots received after election day had to be set aside and not included in the vote count.

This year, in Texas in the middle of a pandemic, the Governor ruled that each county could only have one drop-box. Now, some counties in Texas are bigger than some states in the US, and guess who has less access to transportation? On top of the Governor's ruling, there was a lawsuit to throw out votes cast in drive-through locations. The Texas State Supreme Court rejected the lawsuit TWO DAYS before election day; the federal court will make a ruling today...the DAY BEFORE the election day.

We are still fighting for our right to vote. We still fight for freedom.

The process of writing this book has helped me come to terms with some issues that I've struggled with. I've realized that as painful as it was, the time that I spent in quarantine was also a huge blessing. It gave me access to love and support that I had never experienced until I met my teacher, Miss Anderson. She opened the door to learning about myself and the world. Her nurturing gave me the foundation to recognize and accept love, not just for myself, but also FROM myself.

**GRANDPA TONY, ME, NANNY, MY
DAUGHTER LAURA, MY MOM**

Thanks to her foundation, I became willing to embrace
the positive and supportive attention that I received as
I grew up. From Mrs. Williams, I learned the value of
perspective and putting myself in others' shoes. From
Grandma Lottie, I learned to treat others with kindness
and respect, and that my smile has to come from
within. From Mr Knoblauch, I learned to take
responsibility for my words and follow them up with
actions. Their faith helped me to reject the negative

attention that I received from Grandpa Tony and my own Mother.

My Great-Grandfather personally and directly wreaked havoc on four generations of women. He was aided and abetted by the silence of my Mother and Grandmother. My Grandmother's shame gave him unsupervised access to my Mother, and her shame gave him unsupervised access to me. I did not share their sense of shame when he put his hands on me, but their willingness to protect him at my expense left me feeling lonely, lost, and unloved, which affected my ability to form loving relationships, especially with my own daughter.

I don't think that my Mom received much positive attention as a kid, or maybe she just didn't know how to embrace and internalize the positive. I understand that the strain in our relationship was not about me. Mom was deeply, deeply wounded, and was unable to heal. I don't blame her. My heart breaks for her.

Ultimately, I've learned that forgiveness is all about compassion. I forgive my Mom because I see how damaged and lonely she was. I forgive my great-grandfather out of compassion for myself. I am freeing myself from carrying the burden of the pain he caused. That burden was never mine; it belonged to him alone. I have enough compassion for myself to let that pain go.

I know that I've made mistakes in my relationships with my own kids, particularly my eldest daughter. I take full responsibility. My addiction to alcohol escalated drastically as my relationship with my future husband progressed. She bore witness to that. I sobered up when she was six- years-old.

In my guilt and my desire to have a better connection than what I had with my own Mom, I took it too far. I became more friend than Mom, which created a lot of problems in our communication as she grew into her teen years and needed more emotional safety, security, and guidance than I provided.

I deeply feared her rejection and abandonment. I put more value on knowing that she liked me instead of trusting that she loved me, and guiding her into loving herself. I subconsciously put so much pressure on trying to avoid duplicating my relationship with my Mother that my daughter became a surrogate FOR my Mother, and I deferred to her as if she WAS my Mother.

My daughter couldn't give me what I needed, because what I needed most was my own love for myself. The love that I need the most comes from within me. Only I know what loving me means to me.

I hope that she and I together can build a strong foundation for her daughter, my Granddaughter, and that the two of them can continue to improve on the legacy of connection between Mother and Daughter.

In the end, I also need compassion for myself. I did the best that I could with the knowledge that I had at the time. The harm that I caused was never intentional; still, there were consequences. I have to love myself enough to forgive myself for not understanding how much pain I was in, and how much pain I may have caused.

When life gets tough, I still have those "I want my Mommy" moments. I know that I'm not referring to my actual Mom. My Mom never had the capacity to give me what I needed, and she passed away many years ago.

What I mean is that the little girl in me yearns to be wrapped in the bosom of love. That little girl will never knew what it feels like to receive that loving embrace, but the grown-up me knows what it feels like to GIVE that loving embrace, so that's what I do. I give her the comfort, the safety, and security that only I can provide her.

Life does gets tough sometimes, and when I'm in the shit, I'm focused on survival. My feelings don't matter, and won't get processed until I feel safe enough to be still. That may not happen for years, perhaps even decades beyond the event. Guilt is useless, and guarantees that I'll remain stuck in pain. Emotional pain is toxic if left to fester.

I am not flawed; I am human. And I am deeply loved.

ACKNOWLEDGEMENTS

Thank you to my Mom and Dad for doing the best that they could, and to my brothers: Vincent (Bro), Brian, David, Billy, and my sisters: Samantha and Tracee, for surrounding me with laughter and loyalty.

Thank you to Miss Anderson, Mrs. Williams, and Mr. Knoblauch for recognizing and nurturing the light inside of me.

Thank you to my therapist, Dr. Alice Tindi for helping me see that the cage I was keeping myself in was never locked. Thanks also to my psychiatrist, Dr. Karen Anderson for guiding me to the proper anti-depressant medication.

Thank you to Terri Best, and her Leadership Academy for Women, for helping me find the courage to amplify my voice.

Thank you to my dear friends, Becky Shedd and Lynne Christianson for providing comfort, safety, and unwavering support.

Thank you to my kids, Laura, Zeke, Jake, Roxie, and Ezra for teaching me how to give and receive love.

Thank you to my Glamdaughter, Venisa, for motivating me to be emotionally, spiritually, and physically healthy, for both of our sakes, so that my damage doesn't infect her. She inspires me to model what it looks like to be proud of myself.

ABOUT THE AUTHOR

Veneta Shepherd

Veneta is the oldest of seven, Mom to five (three on the autism spectrum); Glamma to two (so far); widow; 2nd degree Black Belt; special needs advocate; Best Dancer of 9th Grade; former tetherball and volleyball Queen; RuPaul's Drag Race superfan; lover of musicals, sci-fi, and popcorn, non-swimming, hat-knitting blue-haired bundle of fun.

This is her first book.

Made in the USA
Monee, IL
21 April 2021